FOR STEVEN WHO BELIEVED IN ME EVEN AS HE DOUBTED

Introduction

WHAT YOU NEED TO KNOW

Gluten free baking is not like 'normal' baking, you need to forget everything that you thought you knew. Trust me. I've spent thousands of hours perfecting these gluten and dairy free recipes. A significant number are also suitable for vegans (look for the (V)), and for those who are allergic to other foods.

At Twice as Nice we aim to keep it simple so you're not overwhelmed with needing ten new flours and loads of mystery ingredients to bake a cake.

But don't misunderstand, the focus is on what we are putting IN our bakes and not what we are leaving OUT. Our flour mix is unique, unfortunately you can't buy it ready mixed. Mixing it yourself will save you some cash and produce a much better bake than flours that you can find in the supermarket.

In case you were wondering this little book is not a stylish book full of pictures of beautiful people with long glossy hair and trust fund lifestyles. It's a recipe book, and a 'How to' book, it gives precise details of our award-winning recipes. It can teach you how to bake without gluten, milk, eggs and a host of other allergens. What it lacks in style it makes up for in substance.

Confidence: This type of baking is only challenging because it's new. When you get used to making gluten free bread you'll find it's so much more straightforward than traditional wheat or rye bread. There's no hanging around waiting for the gluten to do its thing.

Top Tip: If a batter is runny, that's a good thing. If you can pour it, it'll be fabulous when baked. If it looks like a 'normal' cake batter before you bake it, then you'll be able to use it to build walls or throw at unwelcome visitors after baking. If that's what you're looking for in a cake then go ahead and attempt to make a GF cake in the same way as a gluten one. This is even more relevant for bread.

Caution: If you're new to Gluten free (GF) and Dairy Free (DF) baking and your bakes do have to be 100% GF/DF make sure that you use separate equipment (bowls, spoons, tins, etc). The legal definition for gluten free in Europe is less than 20pppm gluten which is about 20 grains of flour out of a kilo. For example, a wooden spoon if not exclusively used for GF baking could harbour grains of flour to cross-contaminate your bakes.

Essential: All ingredients must be weighed in grams for accuracy. Free from baking is not as forgiving as traditional, which means that your margin for error is reduced.

Most ingredients are weighed, including liquids. We use the standard T for tablespoon and tsp for teaspoon.

Baking temperatures are in Celsius, Fahrenheit and Gas Mark. If you use a fan oven decrease by 20 degrees, or follow the manufacturer's directions.

TWICE AS NICE (TAN) GLUTEN FREE FLOUR MIX

750g Potato Flour

750g Sweet Rice Flour

1kg Millet Flour

Mix these all together in a plastic container so that you're ready to go.

Why this mix? It works much better than the ready-made blends that you can buy at the supermarket, it's only 3 flours which helps to simplify your life. The potato flour and sweet rice add some glueyness (technical term) and the millet brings wholegrain and a gorgeous yellow colour to the party. See Sources for details.

We also love to use white, brown and whole-grain teff too. The teff grain originates from Ethiopia, it's naturally gluten free it's been dubbed a 'superfood' because of its high protein, iron and calcium levels.

WHAT ELSE ARE YOU GOING TO NEED?

Cornflour for the brioche and Best Ever brownies.

Sorghum flour is the best for sourdough starter.

Gram flour for all our doughnut recipes.

Fine Polenta for award winning Hello Sunshine, Carrot and Courgette cakes.

We use different products as binders depending on what we're baking. For the breads, we use psyllium husk (exception is brioche), for everything else we add either guar gum or xanthan gum.

There's a couple of bakes where we don't use any gums at all. I prefer to use guar, but xanthan is widely available in supermarkets.

EQUIPMENT:

Let's keep it simple...

Loaf tins: 2lb and 3lb

Cake tins are 20cm/8" and 23cm/9" round (silicone is good)

Traybake tin: 20cm/8" square

Wilton Doughnut tins (6 hole) x 2

Stand mixer (not essential, but makes life easier)

Brioche tin (large or small)

Food Processor

Chapter 1

BREAD

When I first started gluten free baking, bread was the hardest thing to get right. I was using flour mixes from the supermarket, and sometimes the bread would look grey. Grey is not an attractive colour for a freshly baked loaf. I went on a couple of courses, and was disappointed to be taught bread recipes which contained egg. This meant that the texture was like cake. No-one (in the UK) was teaching how to make gluten free sourdough.

I was at a brave new frontier of baking. I kept testing and experimenting and tweaking. I had some lovely customers at Rode Hall Farmer's Market who gamely tried my first efforts. With their feedback, and yet more experimentation I arrived at this baguette. Once you get the hang of making your own gluten free bread you'll never go back to the supermarket options... yep, even those 'artisan' ones. Just follow the measurements exactly and you won't go wrong.

(See the video on Facebook and YouTube of gluten free bread with an actual crust!)

BASIC WHITE-ISH BAGUETTE Ⓥ

Makes 6 small

FIRST MIX

500g warm water

2 tsp apple cider vinegar

20g psyllium husk

DRY INGREDIENTS

450g TAN flour mix

5g yeast

8g salt

TO FINISH

olive oil for brushing

Mix the water, apple cider vinegar and psyllium husk together for a couple of minutes using either a stand mixer or a metal spoon. In a separate bowl mix flour, yeast and salt together.

Add the dry ingredients to the wet mix, and either let the mixer run for a couple of minutes or use extreme elbow grease to mix thoroughly.

Cover with plastic wrap. Let the dough rise, covered for at least 30 minutes to an hour. (You can also leave to rise overnight in the fridge at this stage for baking in the morning).

For individual rolls weigh out the dough in 155g balls. You should have 6. For long demi-baguettes weigh out the dough in 310g (makes 3) balls.

With wet hands pat the dough into rectangles about 2-3cm thick.

Fold the top third in towards the middle pressing the join with your fingers. Then fold the bottom third upwards to meet the dough from the first fold, press the join. Use wet hands to form a rough log shape. Gently roll into a baguette form.

Place onto a baguette tray, seam side down.

Let the dough rise, covered with plastic wrap, for at least 30 minutes. Just before baking brush the baguettes with oil and use a sharp knife to make a couple of diagonal slashes on each.

Pre-heat your oven to 210°C/420°F/Gas Mark 7 and bake for 25 minutes (small rolls) and 35 minutes (demi-baguette).

Cool completely before slicing. Cool completely before freezing.

FLATBREAD

One of our customers, Viv, would take these on holiday with her to Turkey!

Makes 10

FIRST MIX

500g dairy free yoghurt

2 tsp apple cider vinegar

20g psyllium husk

DRY INGREDIENTS

450g TAN flour mix

5g yeast

10g salt

1 tsp baking powder

TO FINISH

olive oil for brushing

sea salt flakes

Mix the yoghurt, apple cider vinegar and psyllium husk together for a couple of minutes using either a stand mixer or a metal spoon. In a separate bowl combine flour, yeast, salt and baking powder together.

Add the dry ingredients to the wet mix, and either let the mixer run for a couple of minutes or use extreme elbow grease to mix thoroughly.

Cover with plastic wrap. Let the dough rise, covered for at least 30 minutes to an hour. (You can also leave to rise overnight in the fridge at this stage for baking the next day).

For individual flatbreads weigh out the dough in 100/110g balls. Cover two baking trays with parchment paper. Place the dough on the tray, cover with plastic and roll out to the thickness of a pound coin. Depending on the size of your trays and oven, you may have to make these in a couple of batches.

Let the flatbreads rest, covered with plastic wrap, for at least 30 minutes. Brush with olive oil and sprinkle with sea salt flakes.

When ready to bake pre-heat your oven to its maximum temperature for at least 20 minutes and bake for 10 minutes until light brown.

Remove and allow to cool. Cool completely before freezing.

VARIATIONS:

Before baking scatter cumin or nigella seeds on top.

Add a tablespoon of dried herbs (parsley/sage/rosemary) into your dry mix ingredients.

OLIVE BAGUETTE Ⓥ

We always made these on a Friday, they had a very loyal fanbase.

Makes 6

FIRST MIX

500g warm water

2 tsp apple cider vinegar

20g psyllium husk

DRY INGREDIENTS

450g TAN flour mix

5g yeast

8g salt

30g olives (green or black) chopped

TO FINISH

olive oil for brushing

sea salt flakes

Mix the water, apple cider vinegar and psyllium husk together for a couple of minutes using either a stand mixer or a metal spoon. In a separate bowl mix flour, yeast and salt together.

Add the dry ingredients to the wet mix, and either let the mixer run for a couple of minutes or use extreme elbow grease to mix thoroughly. Add chopped olives into the mixture.

Cover with plastic wrap. Let the dough rise, covered for at least 30 minutes to an hour. (You can also leave to rise overnight at this stage for baking in the morning).

For individual rolls weigh out the dough in 155g balls. You should have 6. For long demi-baguettes weigh out the dough in 310g (makes 3).

With wet hands pat the dough into rectangles about 2-3cm thick. Fold the top third in towards the middle pressing the join with your fingers. Then fold the bottom third upwards to meet the dough from the first fold, press the join. Use wet hands to form a rough log shape. Gently roll into a baguette form.

Place onto a baguette tray, seam side down.

Let the dough rise, covered with plastic wrap, for at least 30 minutes. Just before baking brush the baguettes with oil and use a sharp knife to make a couple of diagonal slashes on each.

When ready to bake pre-heat your oven to 210°C/420°F/Gas Mark 7 and bake for 25 minutes (small rolls) and 35 minutes (demi-baguette).

Cool completely before slicing. Cool completely before freezing.

GARLIC BAGUETTES Ⓥ

Makes 6

FIRST MIX

500g warm water

2 tsp apple cider vinegar

20g psyllium husk

DRY INGREDIENTS

450g TAN flour mix

5g yeast

8g salt

0.75 T freeze dried parsley

0.25 T freeze dried oregano

olive oil

FILLING

1 T crushed garlic

1 tsp sea salt

3 T soft dairy free spread

Mix the water, apple cider vinegar and psyllium husk together for a couple of minutes using either a stand mixer or a metal spoon. In a separate bowl mix flour, yeast, salt and herbs together. Add the dry ingredients to the wet mix, and either let the mixer run for a couple of minutes or use extreme elbow grease to mix thoroughly.

Cover with plastic wrap. Let the dough rise, covered for at least 30 minutes to an hour. (You can also leave to rise overnight at this stage for baking in the morning).

For individual rolls weigh out the dough in 155g balls. You should have 6. For long demi-baguettes weigh out the dough in 310g (makes 3).

With wet hands pat the dough into rectangles about 2-3cm thick. Fold the top third in towards the middle pressing the join with your fingers. Then fold the bottom third upwards to meet the dough from the first fold, press the join. Use wet hands to form a rough log shape. Gently roll into a baguette form.

Place onto a baguette tray, seam side down.

Let the dough rise, covered with plastic wrap, for at least 30 minutes.

When ready to bake pre-heat your oven to 210°C/420°F/Gas Mark 7.

Generously brush olive oil onto each roll. Bake for 25 minutes (small rolls) and 35 minutes (demi-baguette).

While the baguettes are baking make the filling by combining 1T crushed garlic with the salt and dairy free spread.

Once the baguettes are cool, use a sharp knife to make slashes at regular intervals in the bread. Fill with the garlic mixture, wrap in foil and return to a pre-heated oven 180°C/350°F/Gas Mark 4 for ten minutes.

FOCACCIA (THE ITALIAN WAY) ⓥ

We briefly had a genuine Italian working with us. This was his contribution.

Makes 6

FIRST MIX

500g warm water

2 tsp apple cider vinegar

20g psyllium husk

1 T olive oil

DRY INGREDIENTS

450g TAN flour mix

5g yeast

8g salt

TO FINISH

olive oil for brushing

sea salt

0.5 T Dried oregano (OH-Ree-GARN-OH!)

Mix the water, apple cider vinegar, psyllium husk and oil together for a couple of minutes using either a stand mixer or a metal spoon. In a separate bowl mix flour, yeast and salt together. Add the dry ingredients to the wet mix, and either let the mixer run for a couple of minutes or use extreme elbow grease to mix thoroughly.

Cover with plastic wrap. Let the dough rise, covered for at least an hour.

Weigh out the dough in 155g balls. You will have 6. With wet hands shape the dough into balls.

Place onto a baking tray, cover with cling film and leave to rise for a further 30 minutes.

Using a silicon brush, lightly brush each roll with oil.

Bake in a pre-heated oven at 210°C/420°F/Gas Mark 7 for 25 minutes.

Sprinkle with sea salt and dried oregano after baking.

Cool completely before freezing.

FOCACCIA (THE ENGLISH WAY) Ⓥ

One day we tried to explain to the Italian that many English people think of Focaccia as a large bread to be shared. This was the result.

Makes 1

FIRST MIX

500g warm water

2 tsp apple cider vinegar

20g psyllium husk

1T olive oil

DRY INGREDIENTS

450g TAN flour mix

5g yeast

8g salt

TO FINISH

olive oil for brushing

sea salt

rosemary sprigs

Mix the water, apple cider vinegar, psyllium husk and oil together for a couple of minutes using either a stand mixer or a metal spoon. In a separate bowl mix flour, yeast and salt together. Add the dry ingredients to the wet mix, and either let the mixer run for a couple of minutes or use extreme elbow grease to mix thoroughly.

Cover with plastic wrap. Let the dough rise, covered for at least an hour.

Fully line a baking tin (20cm by 34cm/8" by 13.5" by 8") with baking parchment, place the dough gently into the tin, stretching to reach the corners. Cover again with plastic wrap, and let rise for a further 45 minutes.

Dip your fingertips in water and make indentations all over the bread. Brush generously with olive oil, sprinkle with sea salt and rosemary sprigs.

Bake in a pre-heated oven at 210°C/420°F/Gas Mark 7 for 25 minutes.

Serve warm.

Cool completely before freezing.

TEFF BREAD Ⓥ

This is a grain that you need to become acquainted with. It's been dubbed a 'superfood'. It contains iron, calcium and protein which is unusual in a grain. This loaf is one of our best sellers. Sarah an Instagram food and fitness blogger (@the growingbutterfly) would turn this into the most amazing French toast. Mike liked it so much that he refused to let me close the shop until he had the recipe (you can see his brilliant loaves on our Facebook page).

You can either use brown or white teff or a mix of the two. This is one that you can experiment with to see where your taste preference lies. You can even include the whole grain (which is tiny) to give an extra level of nutty flavour to the loaf.

Makes 1

FIRST MIX

520g warm water

20g psyllium husk

DRY INGREDIENTS

75g white teff flour

75g brown teff flour

250g TAN flour blend

3g yeast

6g salt

TO FINISH

olive oil

Mix the water and psyllium husk together for a couple of minutes using either a stand mixer or a metal spoon. In a separate bowl mix the flours, yeast and salt together. Add the dry ingredients to the wet mix, and either let the mixer run for a couple of minutes or use extreme elbow grease to mix thoroughly.

Let the dough rise, covered for at least an hour.

Turn out the dough onto a lightly floured surface and pat into a square or rectangle.

Fold the top third in towards the middle, fold the bottom third upwards. Press the join lightly. Use wet hands to form a rough log shape.

Place the dough into a 3lb loaf tin, seam side down.

Let the dough rise, covered with plastic wrap, for at least an hour. (You can also leave to rise overnight in the fridge at this stage for baking in the morning).

When ready to bake pre-heat your oven to 230°C/450°F/Gas Mark 8. Lightly oil the top of the bread with olive oil and bake for 45-55 minutes. Turn loaf out.

Cool completely before slicing.

If you won't eat it all in a couple of days then slice and freeze.

VARIATIONS:

For a whiter loaf use 165g white teff flour in place of 50% white/50% brown.

For a wholemeal loaf use 140g brown teff flour in place of 50% white/50% brown.

Add in up to a tablespoon of the whole teff grain for additional texture and fibre.

For an approximation of 'rye' bread use 140g brown teff flour in place of 50% white/50% brown and scatter 1 teaspoon of caraway seed over the top.

NÖTTER LOAF Ⓥ

Not-a-Loaf, geddit? Still makes me smile. Obviously, the judges at the World Bread Awards 2015 didn't get it. If they were judging on crumb, there's none. Crust? No, none of that either. This is a nutrient dense nut bread that's flour and yeast free. You can mix it up to include the nuts and seeds that you prefer, just keep the weights/proportions the same and it'll be fine. This is inspired by a cracker that I had as part of a modern tapas meal in Port de Soller, Mallorca. In that skinny cracker, the nuts and seeds were held together with egg white, this recipe uses flax, psyllium and chia seeds as the 'glue'. When I asked the waiter about it the manager came over and said that it was from a Scandinavian recipe, hence the name. So, this is a Scandi-Spanish-Cheshire amalgam which my children call bird-seed bread.

Makes 1

DRY INGREDIENTS

160g sunflower seeds

65g pumpkin seeds

90g almonds

235g gluten free rolled oats

120g flax seeds

25g psyllium husk

25g chia seeds

15g fine salt

WET INGREDIENTS

40g maple syrup

55g olive oil

600g water

Preheat the oven to 180°C/350°F/Gas Mark 4. Fully line a 1kg/2lb loaf tin with baking parchment or use a silicon loaf pan. Spread the sunflower seeds, pumpkin seeds, and almonds out onto a baking tray. Bake until they start to brown. Check after 10 minutes, and give them a shake around. Bake for another few minutes until they are lightly toasted.

They should be singing a little when they come out of the oven. Let cool for a few moments then roughly chop the almonds.

Place all the dry ingredients in a large bowl: oats, seeds, psyllium, chia, salt and nuts. Mix thoroughly.

In a jug measure maple syrup, olive oil and water stir to mix.

Make a well in the dry mixture, pour the liquid into this. Stir well, you don't want any hidden clumps of dry mix lurking anywhere.

Spoon into the loaf tin making sure that you smooth the surface as what you see in front of you is how it will bake. Cover with cling film, and let it sit for at least an hour, if you'll be baking the next day pop it into the fridge.

When you're ready to bake preheat the oven to 200°C/400°F/Gas Mark 6, bake for 45 minutes. Let it cool for 10 minutes in the tin, then remove and leave to cool completely. If you try to slice when it's warm it will fall to nutty bits.

If you won't eat it all in a couple of days then slice and freeze.

APPLE BRIOCHE BREAD

This is the brioche that won a silver at the World Bread Awards in 2015.

Makes 1 large or 6 small

FIRST MIX

150g apple juice

50g hard dairy free spread

40g honey

40g sugar

2 large beaten eggs (2 teaspoons reserved for egg wash)

DRY INGREDIENTS

210g TAN flour mix

50g cornflour

0.5tsp guar/xanthan gum

3g yeast

4g salt

FRUIT

1 small eating apple, peeled, cored and chopped

TO FINISH

1 T honey

Heat apple juice over a low heat with the dairy free spread, honey and sugar. Stir, remove from the heat once melted. Allow to cool.

Combine the flour mix with cornflour, gum, yeast and salt.

Whisk the eggs into the cooled apple juice mixture and combine well.

Make a well in the dry ingredients, pour in the wet ingredients and mix well. Cover with cling film and leave for at least an hour in a draught free location.

(After this first rise, place in the fridge for a couple of hours, it's also fine if you leave it overnight).

When ready to bake, use dairy free spread or sunflower oil to grease the inside of the brioche tin, or you could use a round cake tin, it just won't be as pretty. Very gently pour the mixture into the tin taking care not to be overly rough with all those air bubbles.

Cover and leave to rise in a warm place for another hour. Pre-heat the oven to 180°C/350°F/Gas Mark 4.

Just before you put the brioche into the oven, core and chop the apple and drop into the mixture. Do not stir it in.

Take your reserved 2 teaspoons of whisked egg and add 2 teaspoons of water. Use a pastry brush to coat the top of the brioche.

Bake for 45 minutes. If you use mini brioche tins the bake time will be 30 minutes. Drizzle with honey when it comes out of the oven. Eat when warm.

Chapter 2

SOURDOUGH

Obviously, this should be in the bread section, but I've carved it out as you can quite happily live off the preceding bread recipes. This is here for the Breadheads, for the people who miss sourdough, who maybe think they'll never again meet a crackling crust. Why's it separated out from the rest of the bread? Because it's not for the faint of heart. Sourdough is a commitment, getting your starter going requires time, patience and a little bit of skill. For me this was the most challenging aspect of learning to bake gluten free.

I was an experienced home baker, and loved making wheat sourdough bread (it's still the best that I've tasted except for Iggy's in Bronte, Sydney). When I decided to make a gluten free sourdough I contacted a couple of innovative GF bakers, but couldn't find anyone in the UK to help me. I decided to email the owner of a dedicated GF Sourdough bakery in California. Via email we had a brief correspondence which set me on the right road. In 2015, this basic sourdough recipe won a Bronze at the World Bread Awards, not bad for a loaf baked in a home oven.

Why, you're wondering, should I bother with this sourdough malarkey when I've already told you that it's a faff, and more work to look after than a sulky three-year-old on a rainy day in the Lake District? Well once your starter's up and running, it's brilliant, it takes a couple of minutes of mixing and measuring, an overnight rise, then into the oven. The real bonus is that it stays good for a few days, and makes the best toast.

SOURDOUGH STARTER

Let's get this Starter started! Deep breath, we need a new flour... I know, I know. Just take it from my (bitter) experience that this works best, and will save you time, mascara-streaked cheeks and more drama than EastEnders at Christmas. When it's up and running, you can easily switch it to a new flour.

While you're coming to terms with the need for a new flour, I might as well break it to you that an additional piece of kit is also required. Look, I'm sorry, stop reading now if you're going to be like that. I did say it was a faff... I mean who needs a crackling crust, and bread that tastes like you remember it.

Still with me? Good.

INGREDIENTS

1 kg sorghum flour

1 litre bottled water (that you've bought from the shop, not ran from the tap to a bottle)

KIT

freezer bags (closable kind) Medium size

large thermos flask (I used an Easiyo yoghurt making container)

DAY 1

Measure 50g sorghum and 120g of bottled water into a freezer bag.

Mix, seal the bag, mix some more. Let out any air. Reseal.

Place the bag into a second bag, seal, let out any excess air from the second bag.

Three quarters fill your flask with hand hot water. Put your double-bagged flour and water mix into the flask. Seal it.

Check every few hours and make sure that the water in the flask stays warm. (It's okay to go to sleep... you don't have to set an alarm, just add warm water when you wake up). Humans have been making sourdough starters without hand hot water in water baths for thousands of years, we're just trying to control the process.

24 HOURS LATER

Fish out the flour and water bag, there should be a few bubbles going on, maybe some aromas.

Carefully open the bag add 50g sorghum and 80g of bottled water into the freezer bag.

Mix, seal the bag, mix some more. Let out any air. Reseal.

Place the bag into a second bag, seal, let out any excess air from the second bag.

Déjà vu anyone?

Same routine as before soldier, refill your flask with hand hot water. Add the flour and water bag. Seal, check the water temperature periodically to make sure that it's warm. Console yourself with the fact that it's almost made and you won't have to do this again.

24 HOURS LATER

Take the flour and water bag, and empty half away.

Put your remaining mix into a clean (not sanitised) lidded container (Mason jar or Tupperware). NB: Mason jar is essential for any Instagram photos.

Add 50g sorghum and 50g bottled water to your flour and water mix using a wooden spoon.

Cover loosely with the lid, and leave it on the countertop for a further 24 hours.

After this time, it's good to bake with.

Think of your starter as a low-maintenance pet... If you're not using it and it's out on the kitchen counter, discard two tablespoons of starter and add a tablespoon of sorghum and a tablespoon of water every day. If you won't be baking regularly by which I mean every couple of days, put your starter in the fridge with the lid loose, and remember to discard a couple of spoonfuls each week and replace with an equal amount of sorghum and water.

If it ever begins to smell sharply like nail varnish remover you must chuck it and restart the process. If you see any mould growing then throw away and begin again while humming the Circle of Life from the Lion King.

Why use bottled water? Because everyone's water is different, and we're trying to create an environment which will enable everyone's starter to grow. Once your starter's been alive for a month or so you could switch to tap water. (We kept using bottled water in the bakery as the water in that part of Staffordshire is quite hard.)

Only use sorghum flour to feed your starter. After a few weeks, you could start feeding your starter with buckwheat or teff. Avoid rice, tapioca or other starchy flours to feed your starter.

SOURDOUGH LOAF ⓥ

After your Herculean efforts in creating the starter you'll be pleased to know that the actual bread making process is straightforward. Here's our basic recipe from the 2015 World Bread Awards.

Makes 1

FIRST MIX

20g psyllium husk

460g water

60g sourdough starter (at room temperature)

DRY INGREDIENTS

400g TAN flour mix

10g salt

TO FINISH

1T olive oil

Mix the psyllium husk, water and starter in the bowl of a mixer on low for a couple of minutes. Or, use a wooden spoon and make sure that the psyllium is evenly distributed with no lumps.

Add 50g sorghum flour and 50g mineral water to your starter, stir, cover. Put to one side, or place in the fridge.

Add flour and salt to your wet mixture and stir until the flour is fully combined.

Resist all temptation to add more flour. You'll be thinking that this doesn't look like dough, it's too wet, it's too gooey, etc, etc. Try to ignore yourself.

Put the dough into a bowl. Cover and leave for a couple of hours. (By a couple, I mean anything from 2-5...).

Gently turn out onto a lightly floured work surface. With wet hands lightly shape the dough into a rough rectangle. *

Fold the top third onto the middle third. Fold the bottom third upwards until it resembles a vague loaf shape. With wet hands smooth the top of the bread. Place into an oiled tin, seam side down. Cover with plastic film and leave.

Depending on the heat of the room, you can leave for a few hours (2-4) then pop into the fridge for an overnight rise. Or leave it at room temperature, or leave it in the fridge. Your loaf needs a minimum eight-hour rise. My home kitchen is usually cold so I tend to leave it on the counter, unless we're enjoying those 3 days in the Summer when the tabloids scream that we're in the middle of a 'Scorcher!' in which case I'd leave it out for an hour or so, then pop it into the fridge for an overnight rise.

Another simple shape is a round loaf. With wet hands gently shape the dough into a rough round/circular shape. Place bottom-side down (just think about that for a second) into a colander lined with baking parchment and cover with either a clean damp tea cloth, or one of those plastic shower caps that you get in hotels. Leave for at least 12 hours per instructions above.

LOAF TIN BREAD

Place a metal roasting dish on the lowest rack and turn your oven up as high as it will go. (Unless you have a fancy-schmancy professional type oven in which case you're shooting for 225°C/435°F/Gas Mark 6.)

If your loaf has spent the night in the fridge bring it out when you turn on the oven.

Brush the top lightly with olive oil (if you don't do this, it will look weird). Slash a line across the middle of the loaf just before it goes in.

After pre-heating for 30 minutes, add a cup of boiling water into the roasting dish, and put the loaf tin into the oven. Try to minimise the amount of time that the oven door's open.

After 25 minutes turn the heat down to 200°C/400°F/Gas Mark 4 and give it another 20 minutes. Resist opening that oven door.

After a total of 45 minutes take a look, if you'd like it a bit browner then give it another 5.

Remove from oven and leave to cool.

ROUND LOAF

Place a Cast Iron lidded pot into the oven, it needs to be big enough to hold the loaf. I use a Le Creuset pot. Turn up the oven as high as it will go.

If your loaf has spent the night in the fridge bring it out when you turn on the oven. Just before you're ready to place in the oven remove the cling film/shower cap. Brush the top lightly with olive oil (if you don't do this, it will look weird) and slash a couple of lines on the top of the loaf.

After 30 minutes carefully take out the Cast Iron pot, remove the lid, and lifting your loaf with its parchment paper put the whole lot into the pot. Return the lid to the pot and place in the oven.

Bake for 35 minutes then remove the lid, and bake for an additional ten minutes.

Again, if you'd like it browner give it another 5.

Remove from oven, remove from the pot and leave to cool.

GOOD TO KNOW:

Double the mixture, shape two loaves, bake one and let one rise slowly in the fridge for a couple of days.

PINK PEPPERCORN AND PINK HIMALAYAN SALT SOURDOUGH Ⓥ

This loaf was inspired by one that I tasted in the Bronx, New York on a visit to the real little Italy near to the New York Botanical Garden. It was shortlisted in the Bread category at the Free From Food Awards 2016. Tesco won that year with a frozen garlic bread. I'm still coming to terms with this.

Makes 1

FIRST MIX

20g psyllium husk

460g water

60g sourdough starter (at room temperature)

DRY INGREDIENTS

400g TAN flour mix

1 tsp pink peppercorns roughly ground

10g pink Himalayan salt

TO FINISH

1 T olive oil

pink Himalayan salt

Mix the psyllium husk, water and starter in the bowl of a mixer on low for a couple of minutes. Or, use a metal spoon and make sure that the psyllium is evenly distributed with no lumps.

Add 50g sorghum flour and 50g mineral water to your starter, stir, cover. Put to one side, or place in the fridge.

Add flour, pink salt and roughly ground peppercorns. Mix until blended.

Resist all temptation to add more flour. You'll be thinking this doesn't look like dough, it's too wet, it's too gooey, etc, etc. Try to ignore yourself.

Put the dough into a bowl, Cover and leave for a couple of hours. (By a couple, I mean anything from 2-5...).

Gently turn out onto a lightly floured work surface. With wet hands lightly shape the dough into a rough rectangle. *

Fold the top third onto the middle third. Fold the bottom third upwards until it resembles a vague loaf shape. Place into an oiled tin, seam side down. With wet hands smooth the top of the loaf. Cover with plastic film and Leave.

Depending on the heat of the room, you can leave for a few hours (2-4) then pop into the fridge for an overnight rise. Or leave it at room temperature, or leave it in the fridge. Your loaf needs a minimum 8-hour rise, but depending on the heat of the room depends where you leave it. My home kitchen is usually cold so I tend to leave it on the counter, unless we're enjoying those 3 days in the Summer when the tabloids scream that we're in the middle of a 'Scorcher!' in which case I'd leave it out for an hour or so, then pop it into the fridge for an overnight rise.

Another simple shape is making a round loaf. With wet hands gently shape the dough into a rough round/circular shape. Place bottom-side down (just think about that for a second) into a colander lined with baking parchment and cover with either a clean damp tea cloth, or one of those plastic shower caps that you get in hotels. Leave for at least 12 hours per instructions above.

FOLLOW THE INSTRUCTIONS FOR BAKITY BAKE BAKE DAY

GOOD TO KNOW:

Once you're confident with the basic sourdough recipe the sky's the limit. Here's a few variations:

SPICED SOURDOUGH

Use 350g TAN flour mix, 100g brown teff, 1 teaspoon of caraway seeds for a darker spiced bread.

HERBY SOURDOUGH

Add 0.5 teaspoon dried oregano and 1 tablespoon chopped fresh rosemary, 1 tablespoon olive oil for a Mediterranean flavoured loaf.

CINNAMON AND RAISIN SOURDOUGH

Use 300g TAN flour mix, 100g buckwheat, 50g raisins and 1 teaspoon cinnamon for a fruity loaf.

Chapter 3

DOUGHNUTS

The basic recipe for these doughnuts was inspired by living in the US. Our local doughnut shop was called Coffee An' Donut in Westport, CT. We would find ourselves there every weekend, Bill Clinton was a fan when he was President! Truly amazing doughnuts, but not at all friendly to those with allergies.

Our doughnuts, on the other hand, are free from all 14 allergens that must be legally declared in food products in the EU. They were shortlisted in 2016 for the free from product of the year by the British Baking Industry Awards. The eventual winner being a pork pie...

Our baked doughnuts compare favourably to other gluten free baked doughnuts currently available in a certain high-end London food store. I tried a raspberry one when I was in Oxford street, they had a cakey texture and were much too sweet for me. Just goes to show, you can't believe everything that you see on Instagram.

To bake these successfully you will need a couple of doughnut trays (please see Sources).

VANILLA DOUGHNUTS DUSTED WITH CINNAMON ⓥ

Makes 12

WET INGREDIENTS

100g just boiled water

100g unsweetened apple sauce (use organic baby food)

1 T vanilla extract

60g sunflower oil

DRY INGREDIENTS

200g caster sugar

250g TAN flour mix

30g gram flour (sieved)

0.5 tsp guar/xanthan gum

1 tsp baking Powder

0.5 tsp bicarbonate of soda

TO FINISH

100g icing sugar

1 tsp cinnamon

Preheat oven to for 180°C/350°F/Gas Mark 4.

Mix wet ingredients together in a jug. Mix dry ingredients together in a large bowl.

Use sunflower oil to brush the insides of two six-hole doughnut trays.

Add wet ingredients to dry ingredients. Mix quickly using a metal spoon.

Pour the batter into the doughnut trays filling each indent three quarters full. It should pour quite easily from a jug.

Bake for 13 minutes. Leave to cool in trays for 5 minutes, turn out and dust with a mixture of icing sugar and cinnamon. Serve warm, best eaten on the day that they are made.

MATCHA DOUGHNUTS Ⓥ

These are my favourite doughnut!

Makes 12

WET INGREDIENTS

100g just boiled water

100g unsweetened apple sauce (use organic baby food)

1 T vanilla extract

60g sunflower oil

DRY INGREDIENTS

200g caster sugar

250g TAN flour mix

30g gram flour (sieved)

0.5 tsp guar/xanthan gum

1 tsp baking powder

0.5 tsp bicarbonate of soda

2 tsp matcha powder

TO FINISH

100g icing sugar

2 teaspoon matcha powder

Preheat oven to for 180°C/350°F/Gas Mark 4.

Mix wet ingredients together in a jug. Mix dry ingredients together in a large bowl.

Use sunflower oil to brush the insides of two six-hole doughnut trays.

Add wet ingredients to dry ingredients. Mix quickly using a metal spoon.

Pour the batter into the doughnut trays filling each indent three quarters full. It should pour quite easily from a jug.

Bake for 13 minutes. Leave to cool in trays for 5 minutes, turn out onto a wire rack and leave to cool fully.

Sieve icing sugar and matcha together. Slowly add boiling water tablespoon by tablespoon, mix, drizzle in wavy lines onto the doughnuts.

PUMPKIN DOUGHNUTS Ⓥ

These were also my favourite doughnut! These remind me of Autumn in Connecticut when the leaf peepers come out, and thoughts turn to harvest and pumpkin patches.

Makes 12

WET INGREDIENTS

100g just boiled water

50g unsweetened apple sauce (use organic baby food)

50g unsweetened canned pumpkin

1 T vanilla extract

60g sunflower oil

DRY INGREDIENTS

200g caster sugar

250g TAN flour mix

30g gram flour (sieved)

0.5 tsp guar/xanthan gum

1 tsp baking powder

0.5 tsp bicarbonate of soda

1 tsp pumpkin spice (recipe below)

TO FINISH

100g icing sugar

2 tsp pumpkin spice

Preheat oven to for 180°C/350°F/Gas Mark 4.

Mix wet ingredients together in a jug.

Prepare your pumpkin spice mix.

Mix dry ingredients together in a large bowl.

Use sunflower oil to brush the insides of two six-hole doughnut trays.

Add wet ingredients to dry ingredients. Mix quickly using a metal spoon.

Pour the batter into the doughnut trays filling each indent three quarters full. It should pour quite easily from a jug.

Bake for 13 minutes. Leave to cool in trays for 5 minutes, turn out onto a wire rack and dust with the mixture of icing sugar and pumpkin spice while still warm.

'Dust' means dip into the icing sugar and spice mix until both sides are covered. And, yes we did have a container in the bakery labelled Pumpkin Dust.

PUMPKIN SPICE

4 tsp Cinnamon

2 tsp Grated nutmeg

1 tsp Ground cloves

2 tsp Ginger

Mix all spices together in a small glass jar. Keep sealed.

HEATHER'S DEVIL'S FOOD DOUGHNUTS Ⓥ

Firstly, Heather is the Doughnut Supremo at Twice as Nice. What she doesn't know about baked doughnuts isn't worth knowing. Heather started with us on work experience, and we never let her go because she's awesome. Her bakes are irritatingly good. One day I said, "Heather, why don't we have a chocolate doughnut?" and this is what she came up with. They became another favourite.

Makes 12

WET INGREDIENTS

100g just boiled water

100g unsweetened apple sauce (use organic baby food)

1 T vanilla extract

0.5 tsp espresso powder

60g sunflower oil

DRY INGREDIENTS

200g caster sugar

250g TAN flour mix

30g gram flour (sieved)

2T milk free Cocoa Powder (sieved)

0.5 tsp guar/xanthan gum

1 tsp baking powder

0.5 tsp bicarbonate of soda

TO FINISH

Sweet freedom Choc Shot (or similar)

Preheat oven to 180°C/350°F/Gas Mark 4.

Mix wet ingredients together in a jug. Mix dry ingredients together in a large bowl.

Use sunflower oil to brush the insides of two six-hole doughnut trays.

Add wet ingredients to dry ingredients. Mix quickly using a metal spoon.

Pour the batter into the doughnut trays filling each indent three quarters full. It should pour quite easily from a jug.

Bake for 13 minutes. Leave to cool in trays for 5 minutes, turn out onto a wire rack and leave to cool fully.

Drizzle with Sweet Freedom chocolate sauce. No-one is judging the amount of drizzle that you add.

CINNAMON SPICED DOUGHNUTS Ⓥ

These are for the cinnamon fiend, and yes, another favourite of mine.

Makes 12

WET INGREDIENTS

100g just boiled water

100g unsweetened apple sauce (use organic baby food)

1 T vanilla extract

60g sunflower oil

DRY INGREDIENTS

200g caster sugar

250g TAN flour mix

30g gram flour (sieved)

1.5 tsp cinnamon

0.5 tsp guar/xanthan gum

1 tsp baking powder

0.5 tsp bicarbonate of soda

TO FINISH

100g icing sugar

1 tsp cinnamon

Preheat oven to for 180°C/350°F/Gas Mark 4.

Mix wet ingredients together in a jug. Mix dry ingredients together in a large bowl.

Use sunflower oil to brush the insides of two six-hole doughnut trays.

Add wet ingredients to dry ingredients. Mix quickly using a metal spoon.

Pour the batter into the doughnut trays filling each indent three quarters full. It should

pour quite easily from a jug.

Bake for 13 minutes. Leave to cool in trays for 5 minutes. Sieve icing sugar and cinnamon together. Dust the still warm doughnuts in the sugar and spice mix.

Notes

Chapter 4

BISCUITS

I love biscuits. If I had to choose between a biscuit and a cake... biscuit every time. (If you're in the US we're talking cookies here, not your biscuits which are more like our scones. I'm going to stop now).

EARL GREY SHORTBREAD Ⓥ

In December 2014, we entered these biscuits into the UK's Free From Food Awards. They are fragrant, delicate, and worryingly more-ish. They are not like anything that you can buy in a supermarket's free-from aisle. In addition to the ingredients listed below they require patience and time. They were Highly Commended in the 2015 awards, and on the advice of the judges we've now made them milk free.

Makes 30/40

FIRST MIX

175g TAN flour mix

60g icing sugar

0.5 T loose leaf Earl Grey tea (as fancy as you can get, ours has flowers!)

0.5 tsp guar/xanthan gum

0.25 tsp salt

THEN ADD

100g hard dairy free spread (see Sources)

1 tsp vanilla extract

Using a food processor pulse together the flour, icing sugar, tea, gum and salt. The tea should be flecked throughout the dry ingredients.

Cut the dairy free spread into 5 or 6 chunks, add to the processor along with the vanilla. Pulse until a dough forms.

Split the dough into two, and make rough oval shapes. Tightly wrap the two pieces of dough in cling film and place in the fridge to chill for 20 minutes.

Preheat oven to for 180°C/350°F/Gas Mark 4.

Place a large sheet of cling film on the counter (approximately 30 cm by 50 cm), unwrap one disc and place in the centre of the film. Cover the dough with another another sheet of cling film. Roll out until the dough is the thickness of a pound coin. Use a biscuit cutter to cut whatever shapes you'd like. Using a palette knife gently place the cut shapes onto a parchment lined baking tin.

Roll up the scraps, wrap in cling film and return to the fridge. Put the baking tray into the fridge to chill while you roll out the second disc using the method detailed earlier.

Place the second lot of biscuits into the fridge to chill for 10 minutes.

Repeat with dough scraps.

Bake both trays of biscuits for 15 minutes. Cool on the trays for 5 minutes before moving to wire racks to cool completely.

VARIATIONS:

VANILLA ROSE SHORTBREAD (V)

Increase the vanilla to 1 teaspoon and use 0.5 tablespoon loose leaf rose tea in place of the Earl Grey.

CITRUS SHORTBREAD (V)

Replace vanilla extract with orange or lemon extract and add 1 tablespoon of finely chopped citrus peel to the mix.

CHAI SHORTBREAD (V)

Increase the vanilla to 1 teaspoon and use 0.5 tablespoons of loose leaf chai tea in place of the Earl Grey.

ANZACS

I've been making these traditional New Zealand biscuits for my children for over a decade. I first made them the traditional way (using butter, lots more sugar and regular oats) because it was easier to make biscuits at home than take three children under four to the shops... There's logic in there somewhere. Over time they evolved into the version that you see below (shortlisted in the UK's Free From Food Awards 2015).

Makes 20

FIRST MIX

100g coconut oil

75g caster sugar

20g golden syrup

DRY INGREDIENTS

100g gluten free rolled oats

150g TAN flour mix

75g desiccated coconut

0.5 tsp salt

THEN ADD

0.5 tsp bicarbonate of soda

2 T boiling water

Preheat oven to for 180°C/350°F/Gas Mark 4.

Place baking parchment onto baking tray.

Mix oats, flour, coconut and salt together in a bowl. Put to one side.

Melt coconut oil, sugar and syrup together in a saucepan over low heat. Stir from time to time.

Boil kettle. When oil, sugar and syrup have fully melted reduce heat to low. Mix bicarbonate of soda and freshly boiled water together.

Remove saucepan from heat, add bicarbonate and water to the pan. It should sizzle and spit a little. Stir. Pour this mix onto your dry ingredients scraping every bit out of the saucepan. Mix quickly so that all dry ingredients are combined. Scoop a spoonful of mix, and shape with your hands into a round. Press firmly onto the baking tray using your hand. Repeat until all mix is gone.

Bake for 12 minutes. Cool on tray for 5 minutes, before moving to a wire rack to cool completely.

Yield: 15-20 depending on size

VARIATION:

GINGER ANZACS (V)

Add 0.5 teaspoon ground ginger. (Completely unorthodox but delicious, no-one tell the mother-in-law).

SPICED ANZACS (V)

Add 0.5 teaspoon of pumpkin spice (see recipe by Pumpkin Doughnuts)

TEFF CHOCOLATE CHIP COOKIES (AKA THE SUPER GRAIN) Ⓥ

These are a bit Good Cop/Bad Cop as biscuits go. For a start, they are very much cookies rather than biscuits. Pros: Teff flour has protein, calcium, iron; the oil is polyunsaturated; the chocolate chips are milk free. Cons: There's a lot of sugar. The true beauty of these cookies comes from the fact that after you mix the dough, you can leave it in the fridge for up to a week and bake whenever you need that just-baked, soft, chewy, melty chocolaty cookie. Oh, and these are amazing around an ice-cream sandwich. Use vanilla Swedish Glace to keep it dairy free and vegan.

They are seriously good. We sold them at the bakery in that one week when it was sunny.

Makes 20

FIRST MIX

100g sunflower oil

60g water

100g unrefined golden caster sugar

100g dark brown sugar

1 tsp vanilla extract

DRY INGREDIENTS

250g white teff flour

1 tsp baking powder

0.75 tsp bicarbonate of soda

0.5 tsp salt

100g dairy free chocolate chips

Whisk oil, water, both sugars and vanilla together until well-combined (you should whisk to the point that the sugars start to dissolve). Mix flour, baking powder, bicarbonate of soda, salt and chocolate chips in a large bowl.

Pour liquid ingredients onto dry ingredients. Mix well.

To bake immediately:

Cover bowl with cling film and pop into the freezer for 20 minutes. Pre-heat oven to 180°C/350°F/Gas Mark 4. Cover baking tray with parchment.

After 20 minutes scoop the dough using a dessert spoon and place on the baking tray.

Bake for 12 minutes. Cool on the tray for 5 minutes before placing on a wire rack.

To bake at your leisure:

Place the mix into Tupperware, seal and keep in the fridge for up to a week. Scoop and bake as your needs require or your heart desires.

Yield: 20-ish

AFGHANS

Another New Zealand biscuit, I like these because they aren't too sweet if you omit the frosting. Again, this is a traditional NZ biscuit that I've veganised and made gluten free. Let's just keep this on the Down Low, because what the Muv-in-Law don't know…

Makes 30

FIRST MIX

200g soft dairy free spread

75g unrefined caster sugar

DRY INGREDIENTS

140g TAN flour mix

0.5 tsp guar/xanthan gum

0.25 tsp salt

25g milk free cocoa powder

70g gluten free cornflakes

TO FINISH

Either coffee

1 tsp espresso powder

75g sieved icing sugar

Boiling water

Or chocolate

1 tsp milk free cocoa powder

75g sieved icing sugar

boiling water

30 walnut halves

Pre-heat oven to 180°C/350°F/Gas Mark 4.

Cover two baking trays with parchment paper.

In a large bowl cream dairy free spread and sugar together until completely mixed.

Sift flour, gum, salt and cocoa together. Stir dry ingredients into creamed mixture.

Fold in cornflakes until none remain visible in the mixture. Use a dessert spoon to place 30 mounds of the mix onto the baking trays. Press each cookie lightly together.

Bake for 15 minutes. Leave for 5 minutes on the tray, let cool completely on the wire rack.

You can either eat right now for a lower sugar treat, or frost with chocolate icing (traditional) or coffee icing and place a walnut half on top.

Notes

Chapter 5

CAKES

You can't have a baking book without some cakes. Here's some of our most popular... including one that got shortlisted in the Free From Food Awards 2016, and one that was Highly Commended in the same awards.

VICTORIA SPONGE

You can't have an English recipe book without a Victoria Sponge.
The key to a GF/DF Vicky sponge is not to overbake it.

INGREDIENTS

4 large eggs (weigh them all together, yes, in their shells, yes really)

Use this weight for your sugar and dairy free spread. For the flour use the same weight minus 25g. For example, if your eggs weigh 265g -then use 265g of sugar, 265g dairy free spread and 240g gluten free flour.

Same g caster sugar

Same g dairy free spread

1 tsp vanilla extract

2 T coconut/almond/rice/soya milk

25g ground almonds

Same g TAN flour mix -25g gluten free flour

0.5 tsp guar/xanthan gum

0.25 tsp salt

1 tsp gluten free baking powder

TO FINISH:

jam

coconut cream chilled and whipped with 1 T icing sugar or bought ready made

icing sugar to dust

Pre-heat oven to 180°C/350°F/Gas Mark 4.

Line 2 20 cm (8 inch) round cake tins with baking parchment and grease the sides, or use silicone.

Cream the sugar and butter together until light and fluffy. A hand-held electric mixer makes life easier here. In a separate bowl beat the eggs, vanilla and dairy free milk.

Slowly add the egg and milk mixture to the sugar and butter, beating well until fully combined. This should take a couple of minutes.

Sprinkle ground almonds onto the mixture and lightly stir. Sieve flour, gum, salt and baking powder together. Add to the cake mix in the bowl, and gently fold in using a large metal spoon.

Once fully mixed divide the cake batter equally between the two prepared tins.

Bake for 22 minutes, until well risen and the cakes are starting to come away from the sides of the tins. If they look under-done at this point, rotate the tins and bake for an additional 2 minutes.

After removing the baked cakes from the oven, leave to cool in their tins for 10 minutes and then place them on a wire cooling rack.

Once cooled slice off any peaks that may have formed when baking and spread the cut side of one cake with your choice of jam. Pipe the coconut cream onto this in concentric circles. Top with the cut side/less attractive side of the other sandwich facing inwards.

If you're feeling fancy place a paper doily on top and dust with sieved icing sugar.

CHOCOLATE STOUT CAKE

Okay, if I had to choose one cake, this would be it. It's chocolaty, and gloriously moist and dense. It's got beer in it too. It was shortlisted in the Teatime category of the UK's Free From Food Awards 2016, it was beaten by a Banana Teff loaf, some biscotti, a doughnut, and our own Hello Sunshine lemon cake. This cake is simply not like any other gluten free cake that you've tried. I'm going to stop blathering on and just give you the recipe. Did I mention that there was beer?

FIRST MIX

225g soft dairy free spread

325g soft dark brown sugar

THEN ADD

4 eggs, beaten

DRY INGREDIENTS

225g TAN flour mix

1 tsp baking powder

0.5 tsp salt

0.5 tsp guar/xanthan gum

100g dairy free cocoa

150g dairy free chocolate chips

ALTERNATING WITH

330ml gluten free ale (see Sources)

TO FINISH

150g coconut oil

1 tsp vanilla extract

250g icing sugar

Preheat the oven to 180°C/350°F/Gas Mark 4. Fully line a deep 20cm, 8" cake tin with baking parchment.

Cream dairy free spread and dark brown sugar together until light and fluffy. Using an electric hand mixer for a few minutes will make light work of this. Gradually add in the beaten eggs.

Sieve flour, cocoa, baking powder, salt and gum together. Keep the chocolate chips to one side. Add alternate amounts of the flour mix and stout (no need to measure if you're using a 330ml bottle) beating well between additions. This batter is very runny, and may look curdled. Don't worry, it'll be okay.

Finally, fold in the chocolate chips.

Pour the cake batter into your prepared tin. Bake for 45 minutes, rotate the cake, and bake for a further 30 minutes. If the top starts to catch, cover with foil.

After a total bake time of one hour and 15 minutes, remove from the oven, let it cool in the tin. The top will look a little craggy, that's fine.

Once the cake is completely cool remove from the tin.

Make coconut icing by beating coconut oil with vanilla extract, gradually adding in sieved icing sugar. Keep at room temperature. Lightly spread the icing (filling in any craggy gaps) on top of the cake to resemble the frothy head on a pint of stout.

APPLE CAKE

This is a nice, big seasonal unfussy cake. It's best made with apples from the tree in my garden, but please don't come around scrumping.

FIRST MIX

375g unsweetened apple-sauce (use baby food)

3 eggs

1.5 tsp vanilla extract

120g sunflower oil

DRY INGREDIENTS

280g TAN flour mix

60g ground almonds

150g light brown sugar

0.5 tsp baking powder

0.5 tsp bicarbonate of soda

0.25 tsp salt

1 tsp guar/xanthan gum

2 tsp cinnamon

1 tsp ginger

0.25 tsp ground cloves

1 large apple (cored and sliced thinly, I like to keep peel on)

TO FINISH

Crumb topping

50g flour

50g hard dairy free spread

2T light brown sugar

1 tsp cinnamon

Preheat the oven to 180°C/350°F/Gas Mark 4. Line a 24cm/9" cake tin with baking parchment or use silicone.

In a jug whisk applesauce, eggs, sunflower oil and vanilla. In a large bowl mix flour, almonds, sugar, gum, salt, baking powder, bicarbonate of soda and spices.

Now mix the crumb topping by rubbing flour into the dairy free spread with fingers, when it looks like big breadcrumbs lightly sprinkle the sugar and cinnamon into the mix.

Core and slice the apple.

Make a well in the dry ingredients and pour in the liquid mixture. Scoop the batter into the prepared cake tin. Scatter apple slices on top, sprinkle prepared crumb topping over. Bake for 45 minutes, then check. If the top is becoming too brown cover with foil. Bake for an additional 15 minutes. Cool the cake in the tin, do not remove until completely cold.

HAZELNUT AND FIG CAKE

Okay, so this is another favourite, it's best made when figs
are readily available (and therefore cheaper).

FIRST MIX

125g soft dairy free spread

150g caster sugar

DRY INGREDIENTS

75g TAN flour mix

1 tsp baking powder

0.5 tsp guar/xanthan gum

0.25 tsp salt

100g ground hazelnuts
(grind your own using a
food processor)

WET INGREDIENTS

3 eggs, beaten

1 tsp vanilla extract

TO FINISH

50g chopped hazelnuts

4 figs (halved or quartered)

1 T honey to drizzle

Preheat the oven to 180°C/350°F/Gas Mark 4. Base line a 20cm/8-inch cake tin, grease sides, or use silicon bakeware.

Cream dairy free spread and sugar together until light and fluffy using either an electric mixer or wooden spoon. Sieve flour, baking powder, gum and salt together. Keep the ground hazelnuts to one side.

Mix vanilla into the eggs. Add alternate amounts of the flour mix, and the egg mixture into the creamed sugar. Mixing fully after each addition. Finally fold in the ground hazelnuts. Spoon the cake batter into the prepared tin.

Sprinkle the chopped hazelnuts on top. Place the pieces of fig on top of the cake as neatly or as messily as you like. Press them lightly into the cake.

Bake for 45 minutes. Check after 30 minutes and rotate the pan if necessary.

Remove from the oven, drizzle the honey onto the cake while it is still warm. Cool in the tin for 15 minutes. Remove and slice if you'd like to eat it warm, or cool completely on a wire rack.

HELLO SUNSHINE Ⓥ

This is the bad boy that was Highly Commended at the UK's Free From Food Awards 2016. I'll tell you now that it's a bit of a faff, but it's worth it. We bake these in individual cardboard loaf tins.

Makes 13

FIRST MIX

100g dairy free spread

150g caster sugar

DRY INGREDIENTS

100g ground almonds

100g fine cornmeal

50g TAN flour mix

1 tsp guar/xanthan gum

1 tsp baking powder

1 tsp bicarbonate of soda

WET INGREDIENTS

zest of lemon

200g coconut yoghurt

1 T cornflour

3 T lemon juice

3 T Marmalade

TO FINISH

2 T lemon juice

50g icing sugar

candied peel

Preheat the oven to 180°C/350°F/Gas Mark 4. Use silicone friand moulds or cardboard disposable mini loaf trays.

Cream the dairy free spread and sugar together until light and fluffy. Mix ground almonds, cornmeal, flour, baking powder, bicarbonate of soda and gum together. Mix dry ingredients into the creamed sugar mixture. Mix yoghurt and lemon zest into the cake batter.

Mix 2 tablespoons of lemon juice with the cornflour. Heat the remaining tablespoon of lemon juice in a small saucepan, once warm add the lemon and cornflour and stir on the heat until a paste forms. Scrape all this paste into the cake mixture and mix altogether ensuring that the cornflour emulsion is evenly distributed.

Using a piping bag, put a layer of cake batter into the bottom of each tin (makes 13).

Make a small hollow in the cake batter and add a dessert spoonful of marmalade to the centre of the cake. Take care to keep the marmalade away from the edges. Using the piping bag again cover the marmalade fully with cake batter, using a teaspoon to smooth the tops.

Bake for 25 minutes. Remove from oven.

Once cool ice with lemon icing made by combining lemon juice and sieved icing sugar. Decorate with candied peel.

VARIATION:

Bake in a fully lined 2lb loaf tin, do not include the marmalade as a larger cake is not strong enough to support the interior. You could drizzle with warmed marmalade once baked or make a lemon drizzle (1T caster sugar mixed with 2T lemon juice.)

CARROT CAKE Ⓥ

This cake is vegan and can work around other allergies (in addition to gluten and milk) by changing the type of dairy free milk.

FIRST MIX

275ml soya/almond/coconut/rice milk

0.5 T apple cider vinegar

THEN ADD

80 ml sunflower oil

0.5 tsp vanilla extract

DRY INGREDIENTS

200g TAN flour mix

60g fine cornmeal

1 tsp baking powder

1 tsp bicarbonate of soda

0.5 tsp guar/xanthan gum

1.5 tsp cinnamon

0.5 tsp salt

130g caster sugar

DON'T FORGET

350g carrots grated

50g sultanas or raisins

TO FINISH

100g soft dairy free spread

150g dairy free cream cheese

0.25 tsp salt

Lemon zest (unwaxed fruit)

500g icing sugar

Preheat the oven to 180°C/350°F/Gas Mark 4. Base line and grease two 20cm (8-inch sandwich tins) or use silicone.

Add apple cider vinegar to dairy-free milk, leave to stand for a few minutes. Sift flour, cornmeal, baking powder, bicarbonate of soda, xanthan gum, cinnamon and salt together. Add sugar to the flour mix and whisk to combine all dry ingredients. Grate carrots and weigh dried fruit.

Add oil and vanilla extract to dairy-free milk mixture. Whisk together. Add the wet mixture to the dry ingredients, stir well. Once combined, fold in carrots and dried fruit. If the mixture doesn't easily drop off the spoon, add more milk (tablespoon by tablespoon) until a soft dropping consistency is reached. Divide equally between two tins.

Bake for 25 minutes, rotate and bake for an additional 10 minutes.

Once baked, leave in the tins to cool for 15 minutes. Turn out onto wire racks to cool completely before icing.

Make icing by beating cream cheese and dairy free spread together. Once combined, beat in salt, zest of a lemon and sieved icing sugar. Spread icing between cake layers and on top of the cake too.

COURGETTE AND LIME CAKE ⓥ

This cake is vegan and can work around allergies (in addition to gluten and milk) by changing the type of dairy free milk. It was made originally for a lovely American lady who's allergic to soya, milk, eggs and gluten. I find that the English can be a bit funny about courgette in cake. The addition of lime keeps people happy as when they see the tiny pieces of green they think "Oh, lime".

FIRST MIX

275ml soya/rice/almond/coconut milk

0.5 T apple cider vinegar

THEN ADD

80 ml sunflower oil

0.5 tsp vanilla extract

DRY INGREDIENTS

200g TAN flour mix

60g fine cornmeal

1 tsp baking powder

1 tsp bicarbonate of soda

0.5 tsp guar gum

0.5 tsp salt

130g caster sugar

DON'T FORGET

350g courgettes grated

2 limes zest

TO FINISH

125g soft dairy free spread

125g vegetable shortening

1 T lime juice

1 T lime zest

500g icing sugar

Preheat the oven to 180°C/350°F/Gas Mark 4. Base line and grease two 20cm (8-inch sandwich tins) or use silicone.

Add apple cider vinegar to dairy-free milk, leave to stand for a few minutes. Sift flour, cornmeal, baking powder, bicarbonate of soda, gum and salt together. Add sugar to the flour mix and whisk to combine all dry ingredients. Grate courgettes and zest limes.

Add oil and vanilla extract to dairy-free milk mixture. Whisk together. Make a well in your flour, pour the liquid onto the flour. Once combined, fold in courgettes and lime zest. If the mixture doesn't easily drop off the spoon, add more milk (tablespoon by tablespoon) until a soft dropping consistency is reached. Divide equally between two tins.

Bake for 25 minutes, rotate and bake for an additional 10 minutes.

Once baked, leave in the tins to cool for 15 minutes. Turn out onto wire racks to cool completely before icing.

Make icing using a handheld electric mixer. First beat the vegetable shortening and dairy free spread together for a minute. Once combined, beat in half of the lime zest and juice followed by the sieved icing sugar in stages.

Spread icing between sandwich layers, and on top of the cake. Sprinkle with remaining half tablespoon of lime zest.

PINK CAKE

This is included because one of our regulars, Ann, would kill me if it wasn't. Not literally, she wouldn't literally kill me... I think.

FIRST MIX

190g soft dairy free spread

300g caster sugar

THEN ADD

5 eggs (beaten)

2 tsp vanilla extract

DRY INGREDIENTS

450g TAN flour mix

1 tsp guar gum

3 tsp baking powder

2 tsp beetroot powder

0.5 tsp salt

WET INGREDIENTS

250g coconut/almond/rice/ soya milk

TO FINISH

Pink jam (raspberry or blackcurrant)

Pink icing made with

125g soft dairy free spread

125g vegetable shortening

2 tsp vanilla extract

1 tsp beetroot powder

500g icing sugar

Preheat the oven to 170°C/340°F/Gas Mark 3. Base line and grease two 23cm (9-inch sandwich tins) or use silicone.

Using a handheld electric mixer cream the dairy free spread and sugar together until they become light and fluffy. After a couple of minutes slowly add the beaten eggs and vanilla making sure that they are fully incorporated with the creamed mixture.

Use a balloon whisk to mix the dry ingredients together. Add approximately half of the dry ingredients to the creamed mixture and stir until combined. Slowly pour in the milk stirring as you go, making sure that it's combined. Finally add the remaining flour. It should easily drop off a spoon, if it doesn't add additional milk tablespoon by tablespoon until this soft consistency is reached. Once everything is fully mixed divide the pink batter between the two baking tins.

If you have Ann coming over it's probably best to weigh them and make sure they're equal. Otherwise just eye-ball the tins. Smooth the tops, and bake for 45 minutes.

Check after 30 minutes and see if the tins need rotating.

Once baked, let the cakes cool in the tins for 10 minutes then turn onto a wire rack to cool fully.

Make icing using a handheld electric mixer. First beat the vegetable shortening and dairy free spread together for a minute. Once combined, add the vanilla and beetroot powder followed by 500g sieved icing sugar in stages. Put the icing into the fridge to chill.

Decide which sponge will be on the bottom of the cake and slice off any peaks.

Spread your favourite pink jam on top. Using a piping bag pipe icing on top of the jam (you want to make sure that each slice will have some icing in it, so stripes or swirls work well). Place the second layer on top and use the remaining icing to cover the cake.

Chapter 6

TRAYBAKES

When I first moved to the US I couldn't work due to visa restrictions, it seemed a good time to start a family. But it was difficult being far from home and old friends, with a husband who worked away and a baby that didn't like to sleep. I consider myself saved by my local chapter of the International Mom's Club. I attended a weekly playgroup with an amazing group of women (Jessica, Robyn, Joan, Aarti, Kristen, Gretchen and Shelley). It took me quite a while to find these ladies and between us we figured out what we were supposed to be doing as new Mums.

When we were planning events for our Mom's Club group we realised that we needed to offer food to guarantee that the events would be well-attended. We all baked to a greater or lesser extent, Jess's cakes always had the best decoration without question, others who shall remain nameless would crack open a Betty Crocker box mix. I try not to judge, no, I'm judging. We sliced grapes too (to stop them from being a choking hazard), we were an awesome group of Moms who managed to schedule our monthly committee meetings around cocktail hour. Like I say, it took me a while to find them. This chapter is dedicated to that group of wonderful women now living all over the place (Connecticut, New York, Los Angeles...).

What's this got to do with traybakes? There's three brownie recipes in this chapter, and for me brownies are inextricably linked with my American experience.

BEST EVER BROWNIE

This Brownie has caused me so much trouble. Not in the making of it, that's quite straightforward. But with our customers loving it so much, and being very precise in exactly which piece they'd like. Ann (remember Pink Cake Ann?) would only want a middle piece with no edges. Claire would want an edge. Elliot liked a corner. Viv was very flexible about the location of her slice, but would notice immediately if we changed the cocoa supplier. One Saturday Ann had to have a piece with an edge.... (when I write that sentence, it looks quite innocent) however it took a while for our Saturday girl Izzy to get over the trauma.

This is another American classic which we have made gluten and dairy free. It's very chocolatey because chocolate is the main ingredient. Duh! It's awesome, and I understand why our customers are so passionate about it.

Makes 12

FIRST MIX:

450g milk free chocolate

160g soft dairy free spread

THEN ADD:

175g caster sugar

4 eggs (beaten)

DON'T FORGET:

60g cornflour

2 T milk free cocoa.

Preheat the oven to 180°C/350°F/Gas Mark 4. Line a 20cm/8-inch square baking tin with baking parchment. Melt the chocolate and dairy free spread in a metal or Pyrex bowl suspended over lightly boiling water. Stir occasionally to encourage melting.

Once melted remove from the heat and add the sugar stirring vigorously to facilitate the sugar's dissolving in the hot chocolate mixture.

Slowly add the eggs into the bowl little by little beating well after each addition.

Sieve the cornflour and milk free cocoa into the mix and beat as if your life depends on it. For a couple of minutes, or 1 minute if you've got biceps like Popeye.

Pour into the prepared tin, smooth the surface making sure that the mixture gets into the corners (otherwise you'll be ripping off Elliot, and he won't be happy). Bake for 25 minutes...unless you know for a fact that your oven is dodgy and always needs a few extra minutes.

DO NOT OVERBAKE. I'm sorry if that looks like shouting but every British person's natural inclination is to overbake a brownie.

Leave it in the tin to cool. We prefer to bake it and leave it until the next day before slicing. If you try to slice it before it's 100% cool it will fall to pieces and make you quite sad.*

Voice of experience

SWEET POTATO BROWNIES Ⓥ

These brownies are free from all 14 EU allergens. They also taste amazing. I tried Deliciously Ella's Sweet potato brownie when I was in London and she had a short collaboration with Raw Press in Mayfair. These are better.

Makes 12

FIRST MIX

200g sweet potato (un-cooked weight, baked until soft 200C for 45 minutes, or peeled and microwaved until soft)

125ml sunflower oil

120ml maple syrup

1 tsp vanilla extract

220ml rice milk

DRY INGREDIENTS

200g TAN flour mix

100g cocoa (sieved)

0.5 tsp baking powder

0.25 tsp salt

0.5 tsp guar/xanthan gum

200g unrefined caster sugar

THEN ADD

100g chocolate chips

Preheat the oven to 170°C/340°F/Gas Mark 3. Line a 20cm/8-inch square baking tin with baking parchment.

In a food processor pulse the sweet potato, oil, maple syrup, vanilla and rice milk until a thick orange puree forms (make sure that no lumps of sweet potato remain).

Add the flour, cocoa, baking powder, salt, gum and sugar to the processor. Pulse again until combined. Carefully lift out the blade, using a silicon spatula to make sure that as much mixture as possible stays in the bowl. Add chocolate chips, stir briefly to mix.

Spoon the batter into the tin, bake for 30 minutes. Do not over-bake! It will firm up as it cools. Allow to cool in the tin for 15 minutes. This can be sliced and served warm.

VARIATION:

Add in a handful of nuts at the same time as you add the chocolate chips.

STICKY TOFFEE PUDDING Ⓥ

Let's get one thing straight. Sticky Toffee Pudding always contains dates. If it doesn't, then it isn't. Here endeth the lesson. This is free from all 14 EU allergens.

Makes 12

FIRST MIX

180g dates

1 T instant espresso coffee powder

130g boiling water

DRY INGREDIENTS

200g TAN flour mix

1 tsp baking powder

0.5 tsp bicarbonate of soda

0.5 tsp xanthan gum

0.25 tsp cinnamon

0.25 tsp ginger

150g unrefined sugar

WET INGREDIENTS

120g rice milk

1 tsp apple cider vinegar

80ml sunflower oil

1 tsp vanilla extract

Preheat the oven to 180°C/350°F/Gas Mark 4. Line a 20cm/8-inch square tray with baking parchment.

Place dates and coffee powder in a heat proof jug, pour over boiling water. Leave while you assemble the other ingredients.

In another jug combine rice milk and apple cider vinegar.

Sieve flour, baking powder, bicarbonate of soda, xanthan and spices into a separate bowl. Add the sugar to these dry ingredients.

When the dates have soaked for at least 10 minutes, put into the food processor and pulse until pureed. Add oil and vanilla to the rice milk, stir then pour onto the date mixture and pulse to combine. Add the pre-mixed dry ingredients to the food processor and pulse until combined.

Pour into the lined tray. Bake for 30 minutes, and leave to cool in the tin.

While it bakes make your salted caramel sauce.

SMOKED SALTED CARAMEL SAUCE Ⓥ

Smoked sea salt adds an entirely new dimension of flavour, I would
never, ever return to making 'normal' salted caramel. Never.

FIRST MIX

235g caster sugar

65g water

10g golden syrup

THEN ADD

60g dairy free single cream
(soya or coconut)

0.5 tsp smoked sea salt

Put sugar, water and syrup into a saucepan and turn heat to high.
Stir occasionally until the sugar melts. Do not step away from the
pan. (I can guarantee that if you step away something disastrous
will happen).

Pay close attention to the changes. It will start to bubble, gently
swirl the pan to even out the heat distribution. The mixture will
become a light brown colour which will gradually deepen.

When the smell starts to intensify, and the colour becomes a
deep golden brown (think Hawaiian Tropic, Factor 2) then it's
done. Remove from the heat and slowly pour in the dairy free
cream (you're combining cold cream with hot liquid, so be slow
and careful otherwise it will leap out of the pan).

Stir with a long-handled wooden spoon to make sure that all the
cream has been combined. Add the smoked sea salt and stir well
to fully integrate.

This will keep in a Tupperware container in the fridge for a
couple of weeks, or you could freeze some to make sure that you
always have it to hand.

Pour warm sauce over the still warm sticky toffee traybake.

Serve warm with ice cream.

HAIR-ON-YOUR-CHEST-GINGERBREAD* Ⓥ

FIRST MIX

180g dark brown sugar

180g golden syrup

180g black treacle

180g soft dairy free spread

DRY INGREDIENTS

370g TAN flour mix

0.5 tsp bicarbonate of soda

1 tsp guar/xanthan gum

0.75 T ground ginger

WET INGREDIENTS

170g rice milk

90g unsweetened apple sauce

DON'T FORGET

50g stem ginger in syrup, drained and sliced thinly

Preheat the oven to 170°C/340°F/Gas Mark 3. Line a 20cm/8" square tin with baking parchment.

Put sugar, syrup, treacle and dairy free spread into a large saucepan. Heat gently, stirring as required, until it melts together. Put to one side.

Sieve dry ingredients together in a large bowl

Mix the rice milk and apple sauce together. Add the rice milk and apple sauce to the saucepan and stir together.

Make a well in the centre of the flour mix and pour in the liquids from the saucepan. Mix well, making sure that no pockets of flour remain. Once mixed together add the stem ginger and stir to distribute evenly.

This batter is quite liquid, pour into the lined tin and bake for 55 minutes to an hour.

Remove from the oven and allow to cool completely in the tin. Once cool, slice into chunks and enjoy!

This keeps well in an air-tight tin.

Not medically proven.

DOUBLE CHOCOLATE ALMOND BROWNIE Ⓥ

We take no chances with these... we have not one but two egg substitutes, we have two lots of almonds - nuts and milk, and two kinds of chocolate – chocolate chips and cocoa. Therefore, it's obviously 'Double' chocolate almond. See what I did there?

Makes 12

FIRST MIX

10g ground flaxseed

THEN MELT

80g soft dairy free spread

100g dairy free chocolate chips

DRY INGREDIENTS

140g ground almonds

180g TAN flour mix

140g unrefined caster sugar

1 tsp guar/xanthan gum

40g milk free cocoa (unsweetened)

0.5 tsp baking powder

0.5 tsp salt

WET INGREDIENTS

100g almond milk

1 tsp vanilla extract

50g unsweetened apple sauce

TO FINISH

2T smooth peanut butter mixed with 1T icing sugar

or smoked sea salted caramel

Preheat the oven to 180°C/350°F/Gas Mark 4. Line a 20cm/8-inch square tray with baking parchment.

Mix the flaxseed with 45g of cold water and leave to sit.

Melt dairy free spread and chocolate chips together in a saucepan over a low heat. Stir occasionally, once melted remove from heat.

Mix almonds, flour, xanthan, cocoa, baking powder, salt and sugar together in a large bowl.

Add almond milk, vanilla and apple sauce to the melted chocolate mixture and stir together.

Make a hole in the centre of the dry ingredients, and pour the wet ingredients into this. Mix thoroughly using a wooden spoon until the mixture is fully combined.

Spoon the mixture into the prepared tin smoothing the top as much as possible. At this point you can either bake it plain or add swirls of peanut butter or smoked sea salted caramel (find on page 61) on top and bake. (We even used peanut butter to write messages... clearly, we don't get out much).

Bake for 30 minutes. Cool in the pan.

GAZILLIONAIRES SLICE ⓥ

This is like Billionaires Shortbread, but better for you, so we upgraded it to being a gazillionaire. This is a recreation of a slice that I tried in a café in Sydney. They really like their slices over there. This slice doesn't require cooking. I find that lots of raw slices taste the same... this one doesn't.

Makes 16

FIRST MIX

250g whole almonds

80g desiccated coconut

200g dried dates (preferably Medjool)

0.25 tsp salt

0.5 tsp ground cinnamon

2T psyllium husk

1 tsp vanilla extract

2T water

CARAMEL LAYER

210g coconut oil

125g cashew butter

1 tsp vanilla extract

60g maple syrup

0.25 tsp salt

TO FINISH

125g cacao butter

60g raw cacao powder

1 T agave syrup

Fully line a 20cm (8 inch) square cake tin with baking parchment.

Place all dry base ingredients (First mix) into a food processor and pulse to combine. Add water and vanilla extract, pulse to fully mix. If you can form a small ball of the mixture using your fingers it's ready. If it's still a little dry then add additional water by the half tablespoon.

Put the mix into the prepared tin and cover with cling film. Use the film to spread out the base without turning yourself into a sticky mess. We use a small wooden roller to compress the mix, and get it as smooth as possible. Once smooth, place in the fridge.

Make the Caramel by first melting the coconut oil over a low heat in a saucepan. Put to one side. Then add the cashew nut butter, vanilla, maple syrup and salt into the food processor. Pulse to combine. Pour in the coconut oil via the chute, pulse to combine. It should be quite liquid. Remove the cling film from the base and pour this over. Return to the fridge for at least an hour.

Finally make the raw chocolate topping. Gently melt the cacao butter in a saucepan over a low heat. When no hard bits of the cacao butter remain, take off the heat and add cacao powder and agave syrup. Whisk until fully combined.

Working quickly cover the caramel layer with chocolate and leave in a cool place (not the fridge) to set. Slice as needed and store in an air-tight container in that same cool place.

Notes

Chapter 7

CHRISTMAS

Here's some Christmas recipes which all happen to be vegan. Shhh!

CRANBERRY CHRISTMAS CAKE Ⓥ

The secret to this cake is the addition of cranberry juice which keeps it moist, and the dried cranberries which add a hint of tartness. NB: Use organic dried fruit to avoid the unnecessary addition of Sulphur Dioxide.

FIRST MIX

300g soft dairy free spread

300g cranberry juice

200g agave nectar

THEN ADD

700g mixed dried fruit (sultanas/raisins/currants/figs/cherries)

200g unsweetened dried cranberries

150g candied mixed peel

1 tsp bicarbonate of soda

DRY INGREDIENTS

150g TAN flour mix

1 tsp guar/xanthan gum

0.25 tsp salt

1 tsp mixed spice

TO FINISH

brandy

apricot conserve

marzipan

icing

or, cranberries and pistachios

Preheat the oven to 150°C/300°F/Gas Mark 2. Fully line a 20cm (8 inch) deep round cake tin.

Heat cranberry juice in a large saucepan over a gentle heat, add dairy free spread and stir until it melts. Add agave nectar. Stir until combined.

Add dried fruit and cranberries, simmer over low heat for 10 minutes.

Pour the mixture into a large bowl, add candied peel and sprinkle the bicarbonate of soda onto the fruit mixture. Stir to fully combine. Let the mixture sit for a further 10 minutes.

Sieve flour, gum, salt and mixed spice onto the fruit mixture. Mix briefly, then fold in ground almonds and candied mixed peel.

Pour the mixture into the cake tin, smoothing the top with a spatula.

Bake for 1 hour, rotate and cover with foil. Bake for a further 30 minutes.

Leave to cool in the tin. After 30 minutes use a cocktail stick to prick holes in the surface and pour over a capful of brandy.

Once completely cold you can either decorate with marzipan and icing immediately, or wrap the cake up in baking parchment and store in an air-tight tin for a month.

If you choose to store the cake, feed it with a capful of brandy every few days, but not on the day immediately before you ice it.

Before icing the cake sieve the apricot jam, and paint a thin layer onto the top of the cake. Roll and cut the marzipan to fit, brush with water and cover with the white icing.

At Twice as Nice we took a less-is-more approach to Christmas cake decoration and would use simple icing snowflakes in contrast colours (if you need your cake to be vegan be careful with the colours that you use, we used a vegan icing from the United States). Or, we would add a thin layer of sieved apricot jam to the cake and cover with chopped pistachios and cranberries.

FLORENTINES (ORANGE AND CRANBERRY) Ⓥ

These are addictive and quite delicious. A manager from
another bakery in town was a big fan of these!

Makes 20

FIRST MIX

180g sliced blanched almonds

50g unsweetened dried cranberries

40g gluten free flour

0.5 tsp guar/xanthan gum

0.25 tsp salt

60g unrefined caster sugar

THEN ADD

40g dairy free spread

0.5 tsp orange extract

1 T maple syrup

1 T single dairy free cream

1 tsp vanilla extract

TO FINISH

100g dairy free chocolate

Preheat oven to 140°C/280°F/Gas Mark 1. Flatten out 20 silver foil tart cases.

Roughly chop half of the almonds, place into a bowl with the unchopped nuts, cranberries, flour, gum, salt and sugar. Mix the dry ingredients together.

Melt the dairy free spread over a low heat in a small saucepan. When melted add the maple syrup and dairy free cream. Stir well. Remove from the heat add the vanilla and orange. Stir.

Pour the wet mix onto the dry mix and stir until combined. Make sure that it's cool enough to handle.

Place a dessert spoonful into each flattened foil tart case until all the mixture is used.

Then use a teaspoon to flatten out the biscuits as much as you can. (They will spread in the oven giving you perfect little circles).

Bake for 15 minutes, rotate the tray and bake for a further 5 minutes.

Remove from the oven and allow to cool in the foil cases. Once fully cool, melt the dairy free chocolate in a saucepan over a low heat and dip each Florentine into the chocolate.

Keep your handy-dandy flattened foil cases for next time.

Use a fork to make wavy patterns on the back of each little cookie.

PEPPERMINT BARK ⓥ

Weirdly this peppermint chocolate reminds me of Christmas almost more than anything else. I say weirdly as it's not something that I grew up with, I first encountered it in the US and became hooked. It's incredibly more-ish.

FIRST MELT

300g dark dairy free chocolate

0.5 tsp peppermint extract

150g white dairy free chocolate

2 striped candy canes (vegan)

Line a 20cm/8-inch baking tin with baking parchment. Melt dairy free chocolate, add peppermint extract. Stir and pour into the prepared tin. Leave to cool (not in the fridge).

Meanwhile smash up two candy canes into different sized splinters and crumbs. Melt the white chocolate, and pour over the dark chocolate when it's set.

Scatter the candy cane on top and leave to cool.

Once cool slice into pieces. These make lovely little gifts.

Notes

Chapter 8

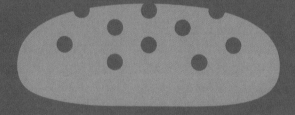

RANDOM ITEMS

This section includes a few of the things that we used to make that don't fit into any of the other categories. Including the North Staffordshire classic oatcakes (not to be confused with those cardboardy Scottish types).

OATCAKES

Staffordshire Oatcakes... the breakfast of champions! These were incredibly popular in the shop, and almost caused riots at Christmas time. Just don't ask. I still bear the emotional scars.

Makes 16

FIRST MIX

250g oat flour (or you could grind oats in a food processor)

250g TAN flour mix

0.5 bicarbonate of soda

1 tsp xanthan gum

1 tsp salt

4g yeast

Mix all the dry ingredients together using a balloon whisk. Slowly add 950ml of tepid water to the bowl, whisking as you go. Cover and leave in a draught free location for an hour or so. Alternatively, pop into the fridge for the next day.

The next day heat a frying pan and add your fat of choice, after five minutes add a ladleful of the oatcake batter, swirl around the pan, and perhaps help it to spread using the back of a spoon. Once the edges have started to go lacy and the top is dry, flip it using an egg slice.

Cook through until the other side is equally brown.

Keep warm in the oven covered in a clean tea towel, while you make the next one.

SCONES

We had a few different versions of scones, this was the most popular.

Makes 10-12

FIRST MIX

260g coconut/rice/soya/ almond milk

1 tsp apple cider vinegar

THEN ADD

500g TAN flour mix

1 tsp bicarbonate of soda

2 tsp cream of tartar

1 tsp guar/xanthan gum

1 tsp salt

125g hard dairy free spread

40g caster sugar

FOLLOWED BY

1 egg (beaten)

Preheat the oven to 200°C/400°F/Gas Mark 6. Cover a large baking tray in parchment.

Mix the milk with the apple cider vinegar, leave to sit on one side.

Whisk the flour, bicarbonate of soda, cream of tartar, gum and salt together. Add the dairy free spread in small cubes. Rub the butter into the flour mix until it looks like large breadcrumbs.

Sprinkle in the sugar, and lightly stir.

Reserve a tablespoon of beaten egg. Add the rest to the milk and vinegar mixture. Whisk.

Make a well in the middle of the dry ingredients. Pour in the milk mixture, and mix gently to make a moist dough.

Turn the dough out onto a floured surface, and knead gently until it comes together. Pat into a rectangle approximately 3cm (1 inch) high. (The dough will be too soft to roll out using a rolling pin).

Dip the edge of your cutter (6cm/2.5inch) into the flour and gently press out the scones. Keep going until you've used all the dough. Add a splash of dairy free milk to the reserved egg, and brush the tops of the scones.

Bake for 12-14 minutes until golden and risen. Eat while warm.

FRUIT CRUMBLE Ⓥ

This basic crumble mix goes with any fruit combination. This was a favourite in the shop.

Makes enough for 6

FRUIT

500g rhubarb

0.5 tsp ginger

2 T caster sugar

FIRST MIX

50g coconut oil

60g maple syrup

1 tsp vanilla

140g ground almonds

200g gluten free oats

Preheat the oven to 180°C/350°F/Gas Mark 4.

Start by washing the rhubarb, and cutting into 3cm/1inch pieces. Add the sugar and ginger, stir to coat. Bake in an ovenproof dish for 30 minutes.

While the fruit is baking melt the coconut oil. Place the almonds and oats in a bowl, make a well and add the maple syrup, vanilla and oil. Stir to combine.

Carefully place the crumble mixture onto the baked fruit, and return to the oven for an additional 30 minutes.

Serve while warm.

MILK FREE MILKSHAKES Ⓥ

These milkshakes would fool anyone into thinking that they were 'normal' dairy ones. Clearly these are not baked, but they are included as they were always popular, especially on the weekend, especially the chocolate one for Reece.

VANILLA

Makes 1

300g Koko coconut milk

1 tsp vanilla extract

75g Swedish Glace vanilla ice cream

Blend all items together. That's it!

CHOCOLATE

Makes 1

300g Koko coconut milk

1 T Sweet Freedom Choc Shot

75g Swedish Glace chocolate ice cream

1 TAN Brownie

Blend all items together.

STRAWBERRY

Makes 1

300g Koko coconut milk

1 tsp vanilla extract

75g Swedish Glace vanilla ice cream

100g strawberries, hulled and halved

Blend all items together.

BANANA

Makes 1

300g Koko coconut milk

1 tsp vanilla extract

75g Swedish Glace vanilla ice cream

1 frozen banana

Blend all items together.

Chapter 9

SOURCES

WHERE TO FIND HARD TO FIND INGREDIENTS.

Beetroot Powder: Local health food shop or www.healthysupplies.co.uk

Chocolate: Plamil is the best source of allergen free chocolate that is also certified vegan. For most of our bakes, we use the Free From Baking Chocolate. If we're not using refined sugar we use the chocolate sweetened with coconut nectar. (www.plamil.com)

Cocoa: In the UK Asda and Sainsbury's own brands are milk free. If the label says, "May contain..." it doesn't come through the door.

Coconut cream: Marks & Spencer chilled and ready to go.

Dairy free cream: Alpro, Soya or Coconut. Available at any large supermarket both chilled and UHT.

Doughnut pans: Made by Wilton, find on www.Amazon.co.uk

Earl Grey Tea: Adagio

Flour: Shipton Mill in the UK, Bob's Red Mill in the United States

Gluten Free oats: Mornflake (based in Cheshire!)

Guar Gum: Shipton Mill

Hard dairy free spread: Stork for Pastries and Biscuits

Psyllium husk: Just Ingredients (Amazon.co.uk)

Soft Dairy free spread: **Pure Sunflower variation (UK), Earth Balance (US)**

Stout: **Greens Gutsy Dark Ale**

Sunflower oil: **Flora**

Vanilla Extract: **Nielsen Massey**

Vegetable Shortening: **Trex**

Xanthan gum: **Dove's Farm**

Yeast: **Dove's Farm**

ACKNOWLEDGEMENTS

Thanks to my Mum and Dad for telling me that I was wasting my time in retail. Thanks to Bethan who valiantly tried to keep me on the straight and narrow whenever I missed a deadline. Thanks to my three lovely children for making me bake when I absolutely didn't want to. Thanks to all the ladies who worked so hard in the shop: Heather – for keeping us on the straight and narrow, Doughnut Heather – for baking up a storm, Izzy – for selling up a storm and making us laugh, and Wendy – for decorating her little socks off. Thanks to you for buying and reading this book.

Feel free to contact me on Twitter: twiceasnicebake or Facebook twiceasnice.uk with any questions or doubts.

ABOUT THE AUTHOR

Laura's lived in France, the United States, Australia and Singapore. Few people know that she won the school prize for Home Economics (Food) in 1989. She's passionate about making cake for people who can't normally eat cake.

Find out more at www.twiceasnicebakery.com

Photo credit: Georgie Krippner

RECIPES

33971826R00051

Printed in Poland
by Amazon Fulfillment
Poland Sp. z o.o., Wrocław